Live Life to the Fullest

Enjoying the life God intended

for you to live

By

Darrell A. Case

Proverbs 11:30

Leaning Tree Christian Publishers

Post Office Box 6124 * Terre Haute, IN 47802

All Scripture quotations are from

The King James Bible.

Library of Congress Control Number: 2010902803

Printed in the United States of America

For Connie,

My wife, friend, partner for life

My lover, my little flower

Contents

Acknowledgements

Though a writer's life may be a lonely profession, no one who publishes a book does it by themselves. We may speak of self-publishing, yet this isn't true. It takes the dedication of many to see the completion. This book is no exception.

My thanks to my dear wife; Connie, who typed, corrected, typed, and corrected again; to my editor and friend, Tim Woodward; Mike Brewer, who did an excellent job of putting my jumbles together and printing the final product; and Justin Davis from Davis Design for the cover art. We made it guys, now let's pray God uses this book for His glory.

Image: compliments of djcodrin / FreeDigitalPhotos.net

What does God think of you?

Foreword

Is it possible to live a happy life in this day of stress, violence and depression? Can we have peace when the entire world around us seems to be coming apart? Can we spend our years on earth enjoying the blessings of God or were His promises just for a simpler time? Can we live on the mountain top or are we destined to just survive in the valley?

Some well-meaning Christians declare "if you are not going through problems right now, hold on, you soon will be." Others go as far as to proclaim "If you are not having trouble in your life, you're not right with God."
Several years ago I visited a church in a nearby city. The pastor was known as a godly man and a prayer warrior. As we spoke about life in general, he said, "We're not supposed to enjoy life, are we?"

To him it was a rhetorical question; unfortunately most Christians hold this same view. They believe in Christ, He is their savior. They love Him with all their heart. Their future home is in heaven, they attend church each Sunday and most mid- week services. They endeavor to raise their children in the nurture and admonition of the Lord. They witness to friends and family, yet to them, life is something to endure.

They are like the small orphan boy adopted by a well-to-do family from a poor orphanage. The child reveled in the luxury of his own room. Sleeping in such a wonderful bed was a dream come true. He awoke the next morning to the sun streaming in his open window. The songs of birds welcomed him to a beautiful summer day. As he came down to breakfast, he saw a place was set for him at the large table in the dining room. Fine china and silverware gleamed in the light of the expensive chandelier.

At his plate set a large glass of milk filled to the brim. At the orphanage each child would drink from the glass only so far then pass it on. This continued until the glass was empty. The glass was then refilled and passed to the next child.

With big eyes the little child looked at his new mother.

"Please, ma'am, how deeply may I drink?"

With tears in her eyes, his mother said "Drink it all son, it's all for you."

I believe God has given us the cup of life filled to the brim and overflowing. God says, "Drink it all, my child, it's all for you."

Many Christians believe life is drudgery. Therefore they miss the real pleasures God has intended for His children. His word promises us abundant life.

Albert Einstein said, "There are only two ways to live your life. One is as though nothing is a miracle. The other is as though everything is a miracle."

We can choose to view everything as a miracle from God.

Will there be sorrows? Of course. Will we suffer difficult setbacks? Undoubtedly. Are there enemies of Christians and the Lord? Surely. Does this mean God has changed His mind or abandoned us? No. In this book we will discuss ways of enjoying living on God's blessings. You can indeed *"live life to the fullest."*

Chapter 1

Seeing yourself as God sees you.

What does God think of you? Does He even know you exist? Or is He so busy His thoughts never even touch you? Are you a valueless member of His society, someone who doesn't count? A disposable person?

Today in our country we have "throw away people." Abortion clinics operate at full throttle killing millions of children. Homeless people wander our streets ignored by the harried throngs. Depression rides teenagers until they take their own lives or the lives of others. Some lash out in pain at parents, teachers or classmates. Others draw within themselves.

Our jails and prisons burst at the seams without an end in sight. Law enforcement holds warrants waiting for new jails to be built so they may serve them. Millions endeavor to blot out life's pain with drugs, alcohol or mindless sex. Others immerse themselves in their careers hoping to dull their conscience. Each day thousands of families are ripped apart in divorce courts. Without hope and peace, millions believe they only exist to be tortured by a God who hates them. Any pleasure they have is short lived.

Is it possible God truly does love us? If so, how does He see us? God says His thoughts are only for our good. 'Then shall ye call upon me, and ye shall go and pray unto me, and I will hearken unto you," Jeremiah 29:12.

As a child of God.

The Bible declares in John 1:12 those who receive Christ become the children of God.

As God's children, we are open to all kinds of opportunities. One of the most important is when we accept His son as our savior, we become God's responsibility. Just as a virtuous father acknowledges responsibility for his newborn child, so the living God assumes responsibility for His children. God not only saves our soul from hell, He gives us the wonderful opportunity to live for Him while here on earth. What father, watching his child sleep, doesn't feel his heart swell with love and pride? If called upon, this man would gladly give up his life for his child. In this same way, Christ gave His life for us so we can spend eternity with Him.

This assures us of a home in heaven, and also peace in our hearts. In Psalm 46, the psalmist says, "God is our refuge, a very present help in trouble." When we need the Lord, He is there. As this loving father stands over the cradle watching his child sleep, so our God watches over us.

Some teach if we sin, God will leave us. They believe the God who promised to never leave us or forsake His children; will send them to hell for sinning. Yet who determines which sin sends me or you to hell? Is it God, myself, or some third party? Remember the Bible says the thought of foolishness is sin. Also, whatsoever is not of faith is sin. Will a wrong thought send us to hell? What about worrying over monthly bills? When God said He would give us eternal or everlasting life, was this a true statement? Surely we would never accuse God of lying; if we did, this would be a foolish thought.

Of course God's word is true. As the Lord has said, "let God be true and every man a liar." In other words, He is saying if every man on earth became liars, God would continue to be true to His word. (Romans 3:3-4.)

Salvation makes you a child of God.

Once you were a child of Satan, an enemy of God. In Romans 10:13, the Lord states "Whosoever shall call upon the name of the Lord shall be saved." It doesn't say if you're wealthy or famous or well–educated, the right color or the right ethnic group. The only qualification is for you to realize you are a sinner in need of the Savior. The moment you call on the Lord, you pass from death to eternal life with God.

More valuable than the world.

How valuable are you? Our courts award millions to those who have lost limbs in accidents. Hands, arms, legs or feet have material value; however, no sane person would sever even his smallest finger for compensation.

Some employers believe the way to motivate their employees is to convince the person they are disposable and can easily be replaced. This causes stress and uncertainty for the employee on the job and in their home. Strife results between husband and wife, and children also bear the blunt of this conflict. Instead of increasing productivity, it reduces their effectiveness. Instead of motivating the person to work more effectively, the individual becomes distrustful of their employer. If these company's executives and supervisors could only realize the old adage is true, you attract more flies with honey than vinegar.

If the employee is treated as if they are expendable, they will see themselves as valueless and their job performance will suffer. However, the boss who views each person as an indispensable member of his team will see that employee blossom. Those who treat each employee as a human being with feelings will achieve their goals and the company's bottom line will improve.

3

The child who is neglected by his parents at first thinks he doesn't matter. Then he moves on to self-reliance. Finally, to isolation, believing he can trust no one. Belittling a child will not make that child behave. It only causes him to withdraw from the one hurting him or her. Believing in him, telling the child you love him or her even when he misbehaves will bring him closer to you. For a small child, a hug, kiss and the assurance of unconditional love can cure their present and future problems in life. For the teenager, a smile, pat on the back and the words "I'm proud of you" have a great impact on their life. Knowing mom and dad love them makes a great impression on the child.

Ministers sometimes make this same mistake of stating our unworthiness to God. While it is true we are all sinners, yet God thought us worthy to send His Son to die for us on the cross. It is also true if we fail to do God's will for our life, we will suffer His chastisement. Just like a loving parent who must punish their child, God still loves us.

Moses constantly gave excuses why he couldn't be a leader. The Lord patiently assured him he could. Finally, God became angry at Moses' lack of confidence and sent Aaron to accompany him. Then a miracle takes place as Moses becomes the leader God knew him to be. He boldly stands before Pharaoh demanding the release of God's people. Later the children of Israel are blocked by the Red Sea in front and obstacles on either side. The Egyptian army is coming up behind, there seems to be no way out.

Moses stands up and boldly shouts, "Stand still and see the salvation of the Lord." God opens the Red Sea. Moses leads the people across on dry ground and into history. A pastor friend jokingly said God convinced Moses he could speak and then couldn't shut him up. Would we discount Moses, could we say he was worthless in God's sight? Of course not, yet there are those reading these words who believe not only are they worthless but hated by the very God who loves them. We tend to forget Moses was a murderer and a fugitive for 40 years.

As a future ruler in His kingdom.

People, both Christian and non Christians alike love fairy tales. Stories of the handsome prince or the beautiful princess fascinate us. Even as grown ups, we are thrilled when a commoner is selected by a prince or king. In a very real sense, this is what happened to us. In Revelation 1:6, God calls us kings and priests. Paul said if we suffer with Him, we shall also reign with Him.

Every young prince or princess must undergo many years of tutorage to learn how to proper conduct themselves. No child is born with the knowledge of leadership. Should we whine and complain when the test and trials become difficult? God is grooming His children to reign with His Son. Perhaps today the Lord will appear to take us home to be with Him. When He comes, we will celebrate the marriage supper of the Lamb. During this period there will be a great tribulation on earth.

After this, we will return with Him to reign on earth a thousand years. Our bodies will be glorified, never to feel pain, distress or death. Do you feel your training will never end? Hold on, dear saint, Christ is at the door.

In Genesis, we read of Joseph being a perfect example of a ruler in training. He was hated by his brothers, sold as a slave to a caravan, in Egypt sold again to Potiphar, a captain of Pharaoh. This teenage boy kept his faith in God even in slavery. Joseph's life seemed to be improving. Recognizing his ability and favor with God, Potiphar put Joseph in charge of all his holdings. Potiphar's morally bankrupt wife sees this young man as an opportunity to cheat on her husband. However, she never met a man like Joseph. Instead of giving into temptation, he says ," How can I do this evil in the sight of God?" He runs from the house, leaving his coat. Rebuffed and angry, she accuses Joseph of attempted rape. Potiphar believes his wife (big mistake; if she cheated once, she will do it again) and throws Joseph into prison without a trial. This young man could have blamed God. He could have given up. We have a tendency to believe the people in the Bible were super saints. After all his family had betrayed him, his master's wife lied about him and now in spite of all the good he did, he sets in a prison cell.

We forget the people in the Bible were just men and women touched by God. Perhaps Joseph wept his first night in prison. I'm sure he faced many days of despair. Each morning he rose from his pallet with the prayer on his lips, "Lord, take me out of this prison." God's answer of "Not yet" must have been very hard to take. Yet his true character showed through. Even in Pharaoh's dungeon, Joseph rises to the top. Finally, after several years, he is released to become the second ruler in Egypt. In this capacity, he saves his family from starvation and becomes the ruler God knew he could be.

Later, after his father's death, his brothers fear he will take revenge on them. His answer is classic. "You meant it for evil, but God meant it for good."

If we could learn from Joseph, the end is not the end when God is in charge. Are you going through trials at this time? Perhaps you just found out you have cancer or some other devastating disease. Has a loved one passed away? Perhaps you have lost your source of income. Are you a victim of a crime or incarcerated yourself? Lean on the Lord. Trust in His word. He is preparing you to rule with Him.

As one of a kind.

No two persons are identical. DNA can and has been used to release the incarcerated and convict the guilty. Fingerprints, dental records and hair follicles are used to identify individuals. In this same way, God has made each one of us unique. Also, He deals with each one of us in a distinct way. To one, He allows physical trials, to another, mental difficulty, others may experience financial problems. Did you ever question why? Why is He letting these things come upon me? The old standby question is, 'If God loves me why is He letting all these things happen to me?" Some believe, as stated before, God is an ogre and enjoys tormenting humans. However, it is because of His deep love for us. God wants us to trust Him fully throughout our lifetime; He desires a close relationship with each person.

As a man or woman of God.

How do you see yourself? When you look in the mirror, what is the person like looking back at you? Are they a good individual? Do you like what you see? Is The Lord Jesus Christ your saviour? If so, I can unequivocally say you are a man or woman of God.

You may say, "You don't know the things I've done, I'm not what I should be, I'm for sure not what I want to be." This is true in each of our lives. No matter how closely we walk with the Lord, there is always room for improvement. Our salvation depends on Christ, not on the things we have done or will do. Many people feel they must keep themselves saved. The problem is, this is an impossible task. We couldn't save ourselves; therefore we can't keep ourselves saved. However, if my salvation depended on the works I performed, I would have to ask myself two questions: how long and how much would I have to work? If I worked for two years on a distant mission field, would that be enough? How long would I need to work? For five? Ten? Twenty years? What if I missed heaven by a month, a day or an hour?

Thank God my salvation and home in heaven doesn't depend on me, but Christ who shed His blood on the cross to pay for my sins.

My fellowship with the God of the universe is another story. If I sin, the sweet fellowship I have with my Heavenly Father is broken. It will remain so until I confess that sin, getting my heart right with Him. He is still my Father and I am still His son. Yet the communion with Him is broken. It can only be repaired by my getting my heart right with Him. When the prodigal son left home in the 15th chapter of Luke, he lost the fellowship with his father and the family. However, he was never separated from his father's love. When the son came back home, his father welcomed him with open arms.

Some believe this assurance of salvation gives them the right to do anything they please. Nothing could be further from the truth. If you are truly born again, your heart is changed. If the love for and from God has penetrated your heart, you will no longer want to go back to your old ways. You are a child of God. You are His responsibility.

Just as it is the duty of any parent to discipline and guide their child; so this is something God our Father takes very seriously, as should we.

Notes

_____

_____

_____

_____

_____

_____

_____

_____

_____

_____

_____

_____

_____

_____

_____

_____

_____

_____

Points to ponder

If you have received Christ as your, savior you are God's child! If not, <u>you can be today</u>.

Realize you are, as we all are, a sinner. (Romans 3:23)

Realize Christ came to save sinners. (Romans 5:8-9) Without Christ, there is no hope of eternal life, only a future in hell, Romans (6:23).

Ask Christ to forgive your sin and come into your heart, (Romans 10:9-10 &13) Pray this prayer:

Dear Heavenly Father, forgive me my sins and send Jesus into my heart. I now turn from my sins. I'll live for You Lord the best way I know how. Lord be merciful to me a sinner and save me for Jesus' sake. Amen.

If you sincerely prayed this prayer, you are a Christian and will never face hell, but will spend eternity in heaven, (John 10:27-29).

If you have accepted Christ, write to us and we will send you some material to help you grow in The Lord.

Souls for Christ
c/o Leaning Tree Christian Publishers
P.O. Box 6124
Terre Haute, IN. 47802

Chapter 2

Becoming the person God wants you to be.

You've blown it. It may be you're incarcerated or were in the past. Possibly you have suffered a broken marriage or financial ruin. You can come back; you can be the person God wants you to be. As you read the list below, prayerfully consider what He can do in your life.

Dedicate yourself unreservedly to God.

The story is told of a missionary in Africa. This man taught his son to obey him instantly. One day the child was at the far end of the garden. Standing at the other end the father called to his child, "Son, drop to the ground!" The youngster did so immediately. "Now crawl to me." Unquestioning, the child began to crawl; when he was halfway across the garden, his father said, "Stand up and run to me." When he reached his father's side, the man said, "Now son, turn around and look." Then the child understood the strange commands from his loving father. Hanging from the tree at the end of the garden was an enormous snake. If the child had hesitated for an instant, the reptile would have killed him. His obedience to his father saved his life. In 1 Peter 5:8 we read, "Be sober, be vigilant: because your adversary the devil, as a roaring lion, walketh about, seeking whom he may devour." Satan is ready to pounce on us at any moment. God knows what we need and when we need it. God can and will protect us from Satan. However, He will never force us to stay by His side. Time and again God asks us to trust Him. First we trust Him for salvation (Romans 10:9-10), then He asks us to trust Him for our daily needs (Phil 4:19), and for the direction of our lives (Prov. 3:5-6). With our welfare foremost in His mind, we can trust Him explicitly.

Always seek God's will for your life.

If God wants the best for us and if He loves us so much, shouldn't we seek His will? Yet some believe God's will is so vague no one can know it. Others are afraid to surrender lest He send them to a foreign land. Yet God's perfect will is always best; if he asks us to do something, He is always guiding. He never leaves us to struggle on our own. Whatever His will is for your life, He will be right there by your side taking you through any difficulty. Others ask, "How can I know God's will for my life?" The answer is by seeking and then doing God's will for this day. God doesn't show us His will for our entire life. A man driving from one city to the next doesn't expect his headlights to shine the great distance between the two. He drives the distance illuminated by the automobile's lights. As he progresses, the way opens to him out of the darkness. So God opens our life, one day at a time. Live for the Lord today and He will open up tomorrow.

Don't be distracted by what others do.

One of the excuses people use for not attending church is hypocrites. Of course there have always been and continue to be hypocrites in the body of Christ. A true hypocrite of which Christ spoke is one who isn't saved. They are pretending to be Christians. Others are immature Christians. Yes, they are saved however thus far they have never grown in the Lord. They are like babies still in diapers. The writers in Hebrews 5:11-14 says they "have need that one teach you again." Would any adult want to act like a baby again? Crawling on the floor, unable to converse with those around them, needing someone to spoon feed them. However, we want to be adults able to care and make decisions for ourselves. Likewise, we should never be distracted by hypocrites. A mature, caring individual wouldn't become angry with their spouse because of someone else's infidelity. In this same manner, we should never be discouraged from serving the Lord by what others do. We can't change their lives. Each person must decide for themselves if they will let someone else's infidelity to Christ stop them from living a full rich life.

You can do anything God asks you to.

When God called Moses to lead the children of Egypt, he felt inadequate. Joshua was unsure about his role as a leader. In Joshua 1:2, God matter of factly says to Joshua, '"Moses my servant is dead." He then instructs Joshua to assume command. In so doing He assures Joshua, "As I was with Moses, so I will be with thee. I will not fail thee or forsake thee." With the God of the universe empowering him, Joshua invaded and conquered the land the Lord promised him. In every situation throughout the Bible, when God commanded His people to do any task, He enabled them.

God has a crucial plan for each and every one of his children: go. Go tell a lost and dying world about the wonderful savior. Do you have loved ones who don't know Christ? What about your friends, neighbors? There is no greater joy on this earth than to see a soul who was on their way to hell, bow their head and accept Christ. Not only are they assured of a home in heaven, but will have a new life on earth. The old sinful life is gone; God has given them a new life.

Get rid of the guilt.

One vital element to living a full satisfying life is forgiving yourself. You can't control others; if you ask for their forgiveness and they choose not to forgive you, that is their decision. However, forgiving yourself is well within your grasp. In Hebrews 10:17, God says when He forgives He forgets. To forget is beyond our control; we may forgive, but we never forget. The next time this person wrongs us, our mind automatically remembers. Peter asks Jesus "'how many times should I forgive my brother?" Christ answers in Matthew 18:22, "Jesus saith unto him, I say not unto thee, until seven times: but, until seventy times seven." His reply demonstrates the love Christians should have for each other. Guilt can cripple even the greatest ministry. Paul said in Phil 3: 13, "Brethren, I count not myself to have apprehended: but this one thing I do, forgetting those things which are behind, and reaching forth unto those things which are before." Paul held the coats of those who murdered Steven. With our laws today, Paul would be guilty of accomplice to murder and conspiracy to commit murder. Yet he realized he couldn't bring Steven back to life. What he could do, however, was live for the Lord until he was called home to glory. Anyone who studies the life of the apostle Paul is aware he fulfilled this goal. You can too.

Invest your life in others.

Perhaps this should have been first on our list. Christ made a difference in the lives of those around Him. Eventually, He gave His life for others. Before He went to the cross, He taught us if we want happiness in our life, we must give our lives for those around us. In the parable of the Good Samaritan, we see a priest and a Levite hurrying on to the tasks of the day. No doubt without the Samaritan's help, the wounded man would have died. The Samaritan tenderly washes and binds up his wounds. He then gently lifts the wounded man up and places him on his beast. Walking beside the animal, the Good Samaritan holds the man lest he fall. Arriving at the inn, he carries him to the room. I can envision him sitting beside the bed all night bathing the man's brow until the fever breaks. His compassion doesn't stop there. In the morning, he speaks to the innkeeper, giving him some money to care for the man until he is able to travel. He also assures the innkeeper if it costs more, he will repay him. The Bible never speaks if he was ever thanked for his compassion and generosity. I'm sure this didn't stop him from helping the next person who needed his assistance. At the end of this account Christ says, "Go and do thou likewise."

Notes

_____

_____

_____

_____

_____

_____

_____

_____

_____

_____

_____

_____

_____

_____

_____

_____

_____

_____

_____

_____

_____

Points to ponder

Have you blown it? If so, move on, don't dwell on the past, there is nothing you can do about your past. You can however, change your future. Paul was pressing for the higher calling of Christ (Philippians 3:13-14). Read again the account of Moses in Exodus. Don't let loved ones; your best friend or neighbors stop you from being the person God wants you to be.

Dedicate yourself to The Lord, put yourself into His hands and let Him work through you. Invest your life into others and watch the blessings roll in; write in the spaces above your ideal life. What is your goal in life? A loving spouse, happy children, and a career you enjoy? God and you can accomplish this; let Him have His way in your heart and life. Remember the journey of a thousand miles begins with the first step. Go back and reread this chapter, then write down your first step, your second, third. Soon you will be well on your way to living a fulfilled life. We will be praying for you.

Chapter 3

How to live a successful life.

What is the definition of success? To quote Booker T. Washington: "Success is to be measured not so much by the position that one has reached in life as by the obstacles which he has overcome."

Each year, thousands of individuals pay hundreds of thousands of dollars to learn how to be successful. They travel hundreds of miles to hear a motivational speaker. These speakers make a very good living crisscrossing the country endeavoring to motivate people. Books are poured over by the millions. They are committed to memory, emulated until the next book comes out. Theories are followed to the letter until blown out of the water by the next one.

Spouses are neglected; children are left to themselves in this mad dash for something elusive called success. Birthdays, anniversaries, ball games, school plays are put on the back burner in the pursuit of achievement. For the few who accomplish this momentary dream they find their lives empty. Fulfillment is still an elusive dream. So what is success? Can it be achieved? Does God want us to be successful? If so, does He tell us how to be successful? What is success in God's sight? In this chapter we will explore how to be successful God's way. Hopefully the next few pages we will give you insight into God's plan for your life. The so-called gurus of success cannot bring you happiness, joy, peace and everlasting satisfaction.

What is Success? Money? Fame? Power?

Wealth.

Most people believe if you have money you will have a wonderful life. Surely the large home, the expensive automobile and exclusive lifestyle will make me happy. Some spend their lives searching for the mighty dollar. They work 24 hours a day thinking about riches. Many years ago, John D. Rockefeller was the wealthiest man in the world. He was asked how much money is enough. His answer reveals his insecurity, "Just a little more." How sad this man, who most people believed to be successful, was convinced his life and significance were empty without money.

Others chance their income and sacrifice their dreams on the luck of the draw. They play the lottery each week, sometimes spending $10, $20, $100 or more, trusting in small squares of cardboard and dreaming of the day they hit it big. Fantasizing of the day they will quit their job and begin living. Many become addicted to gambling, losing their employment, family and home. Several have even taken their lives because of despondency.

Those who win actually lose. Within an average of three years, those who win substantial amounts in the lottery are broke. So is money evil? Is it the culprit for all the ills in the world today? In Acres of Diamonds, Russell Cromwell tells about a well-to-do farmer who learns of diamonds. As he thinks on these precious stones he believes himself to be poor. He sells his land, and assigns his family to another. He then searches the world for the wealth he seeks. Finally, in despair, he takes his own life. A traveling priest stops by the home of the man who bought the land. On the mantel of the fireplace, he sees a black stone. He asks the man where he got the pebble. The man takes the priest down to the stream where he waters his cattle. The farm turns out to be one of the richest diamond mines in the world. The moral of the story is two-fold. One, riches can be found right where we are and two, we may not recognize it when we see them.

Unfortunately, many people don't realize that while they are waiting for their life to start, life is passing them by. Life is like a tube of toothpaste; once it is squeezed out, it can never be put back in the tube. With each day that passes, we will never live that day again. The things we say and do can never be unsaid or undone.

Many times, people don't realize their greatest wealth is not in bank accounts or possessions, but their wealth is in the God who loves them, family and friends. The Bible says be content with such things as you have. Does this mean you shouldn't seek a better house? Of course not, there is nothing wrong with providing the best you can for your family. If we believe there is something wrong with material possessions, we would have to condemn the patriarchs of the Old Testament. However, when money or material goods prevent Christ and the family from taking their rightful place in our lives, we suffer defeat.

Fame.

TV programs draw millions watching those seeking fame. Thousands gather at TV networks headquarters hoping to win a chance at notoriety. These poor people shout, waving signs, hoping to catch the eye of the camera for their few seconds of fame. You can see them each day on the morning shows. They stand in the rain or cold for hours just to be seen on nationwide TV.

The actions of film stars are pored over for every tidbit of information. Their every move is analyzed, we hear of their run- ins with the law for drugs, alcohol, child molestation or even murder. Other film stars can't keep their hands to themselves and they're forever running after someone else's spouse. Yet our children count these celebrities as heroes. Sports stars run afoul of the law and are allowed to continue playing with the team. If there is any punishment at all, it is light. They lead lives filled with tragedy.

Power.

Still others believe power is the answer. They follow wealthy business men believing their association will bring them riches. Never mind that the actions of these men are atrocious. Others follow influential politicians hoping they will do favors for them. Some write to celebrities, hoping for a break into the movies, believing these have the power to bring them fame and fortune.

Yet the wealthiest business man is only as powerful as the consumer. If the customer closes their wallet, the business goes bankrupt. The most powerful politician may appear to wield control, yet he is at the mercy of the poorest voter living in the humblest abode. Many a celebrity has found that their fame extended only to the box office or tabloid.

Then who can be considered successful in the eyes of the Lord? It is the mother and father raising their sons and daughters for Lord. It is the men and women who carry the gospel to the ends of the earth. It is the pastor in a small church laboring for Christ, supplementing his income with a fulltime job. In the sight of the world they don't count for much. Politicians pay no attention to them; they will never be invited to the White House. They will never have the possessions like the wealthy or the fame of celebrities.

No, wealth isn't counted by the contents of a bank account. Nor is fame what we've accomplished for self. These dear servants of the Lord may not be acknowledged on earth; they are, however, well-known in heaven. They spend their lives not in pursuit of wealth, fame or power, yet they are the most successful people on earth.

Your Important Relationship with the Lord.

What kind of relationship do you have with God? Are you on speaking terms? Is He just someone you cry out to when you're in trouble? Someone to call when all else fails? Are you one who just carries your Bible to church each Sunday and never reads it any other time? If so, you are missing out on the best aspects of life. A relationship with a Heavenly Father, who loves you, wants the best for your life and gave His Son so you could enjoy living. Some have said there is no instruction book on life or as I read on a billboard, "Babies don't come with an instruction manual." Of course they were wrong. The Book which will lead you and guide you each day is God's Word. However, having the most expensive Bible won't help you if you don't read and apply its words to your life. Cultivate an excitement in studying God's word. Open the pages of your Bible expecting Him to speak to you each day. Many people believe God only speaks in general terms. Go to His word looking for what He wants to teach you today. Is there a specific problem in your life? Then expect God to give you the answer. As stated before, it may not be the answer you want. However it will be the answer you need to complete your life.

Take a stand for the word of God.

Many are falling today, buying any translation which appeals to their eye or doesn't restrict their lifestyle. Yet God always reserves a remnant for Himself, some who will stand like a wall against sin and wrong. Copy and read the following statement every day.

"Fix bayonets"

This solitary command changed the outcome of the battle of Gettysburg and eventually the Civil War. It altered the course of history and brought freedom to a race of people.

For far too long, we Christians have hid sniveling in the corner singing "Hold the fort." It's time to leave the foxhole, do as Christ commanded and charge the very gates of hell. The time has come for us to stand for what we believe. No longer will we hide from the conflict; no longer will we lie on the ground bemoaning our condition. We are in a war. The very souls of those around me depend on our courage. I will stand, realizing the one who stands for righteousness will be shot at by Christians as well as the world. Satan is my enemy, not God. Christ is the one who gave His life for me. He is my captain. I will follow His command. The love of God compels me to love my fellow man and battle Satan even for those who would take my life. Though the forces of hell assail me, I will stand for the Lord.

Have a good relationship with your family.

Many a man has found after he builds a successful business he lost his most valuable asset, his family. Look for ways you can compliment your spouse or your children. Let them know they are the most valuable people on the face of the earth to you.

Saturate yourself with God's word.

The Bible says, "So then faith cometh by hearing, and hearing by the word of God." (Romans10:17). If you want to live a happy life, know what God says in His word.

In Psalms 119:9-11, God urges us to memorize His word. He says this is the only way to keep our lives clean. We can try other methods; however, we will find they are all superficial. If you truly want the best for yourself and your family, you must know how God wants to guide your life.

If you want to live a happy life, make sure your goals are God's goals.

Each person must have goals in order to accomplish anything. The contractor who builds a house or a skyscraper has goals which must be reached in order to complete the project. The designer of an automobile knows they must finish by a certain date for manufacturing to begin. If they fail, they fall behind the competition. In autumn, the farmer plans the next year's crop. He sees the fields full of grain before one seed is in the soil.

Each person will have goals. Unfortunately, most people see themselves as failures. Everything they do, subconsciously leads them to this goal. God has certain goals for your life. Pray, ask Him what He wants for you and yield yourself to His will.

Obey Him explicitly.

If you could hire a psychiatrist, a financial counselor and a personal manager, you would never receive as good advice as you'll find in God's word. No matter how good human advisers are, they can't hold a candle to the Bible. Also, each one would have a personal interest in your advancement. In other words, they would be looking out for themselves. On the other hand, our Lord does what is best for us and for those around us. His love for us has no bounds.

Trust Him totally.

Have you asked Christ to come into your heart and be your saviour? If so, you have trusted Him with your most valued possession. You have trusted Him for your soul, for eternal life. Don't you think you can trust Him for your car payment, rent, or many other daily expenses? God loves you so much He gave His only Son to save you from hell. Yet there are Christians who don't trust Him for their everyday expenses. Some promise God they will pay their tithe after they are out of debt. What that person is actually saying is, "God, if you will bless me with more money, I'll stop robbing you." Time after time I have seen Christians experience financial problems because they wouldn't depend on Him. Yet, I've also seen the opposite. People who have very little income are living very well because they not only trusted God with their soul but also their finances.

Notes

_____

_____

_____

_____

_____

_____

_____

_____

_____

_____

_____

_____

_____

_____

_____

_____

_____

_____

_____

Points to ponder

Who is a person you would consider successful? Why?
What task has this person performed to be viewed as a
success? What have they accomplished for the betterment
of mankind? Do you consider yourself to be a success? If
not, why not? Write your answers above. What can you do
to change? How is your relationship with The Lord, your

family, neighbors, and your church family? What areas need improvement in your relationships? Read Joshua chapter 1. Do you meet God's definition of success? Take action today, don't wait until tomorrow, it may be too late.

Chapter 4

Live a delightful life.

Must we live a dreary life as some believe? No, a hundred times no. Christ said He came so we could have abundant life. I believe this means on earth as well as in heaven (John 10:10).

View each morning as a brand new day. Wipe the slate clean from yesterday. If you blew it, you can't change it; if you had a wonderful day, build on it. As the sun rises, thank God for giving you another wonderful day of life. Thank Him for another opportunity to serve Him. You have 24 hours to live life to the fullest. Immerse yourself in the beauty of this world. God has created the earth for His children, who are better able to enjoy it than Christians? Some believe the world is evil; therefore we should avoid enjoying it.

Others think we are to exploit the world, giving no thought to future generations. Forests are to be clear-cut, not harvested. Animals are to be hunted down and killed without mercy. When someone speaks of our responsibility to care for the earth, they are laughed at.

God does want us to enjoy the earth, using it responsibly and wisely. Yet He expects us to remember we do not own the land, we are only stewards meant to pass it on to the next generation. Children and grandchildren will pay for or benefit from our actions. Let's enjoy the splendor of this world, always mindful of the generations to come.

Submerge yourself in things of beauty; endeavor to enjoy things that aren't necessarily expensive. In fact, the old adage is true, "The best things in life are free." Below is a list of activities I believe you will enjoy.

1. **Listen to classical music.**

   Let the sound waves wash over you. As the music plays, let it cleanse your mind of the garbage we all accumulate. Heaven will be filled with wonderful music, what a foretaste of glory divine.

2. **Take a warm relaxing bath.**

   As you wash each part of your body, feel the muscles relaxing. Finally, lay back in the tub, let your entire body rest, but be careful you don't fall asleep. Throw away your ragged towels and invest in some fluffy ones.

3. **Force yourself to eat slowly.**

   Taste each bite. Chew each mouthful; the faster you eat the more work your stomach must perform.

4. **When you go to bed, relax.**

   Empty your mind of the problems of the day. If you neglect to do this, you will find not only will your problems still be there but you'll be too tired to deal with them the next day. If you have trouble falling asleep, repeat to yourself, "He giveth his beloved sleep." (Psalm127:2.)

5. **Use your imagination.**

   Also, in your mind, picture yourself lying in the shade of a large oak tree by a tranquil lake. The temperature is perfect, the birds are singing, a gentle breeze is soft on your cheek. The sky is a light blue with a few puffy clouds floating by. Soon you will be waking up refreshed, ready to face the new day.

6. Read a good book.

Spend a few moments reading before you go to sleep. One which encourages you and helps builds your self-esteem. The first one, of course, is the Word of God. Some others are Chicken Soup for the Soul. Leave the mysteries on the shelf for another night. This evening we are just building you up.

7. Plant a flower garden.

Don't limit yourself to one kind of plant. God has created large and small varieties for our pleasure. Watch them grow; feel the texture of their petals. Make sure you have a variety you can cut. For years, I feared cutting roses, believing it would hurt the plant. One year my wife gave me five rose bushes for my birthday; each morning I would check the roses knocking the beetles into a can. Cutting off the dead blooms, I'm not sure when I started cutting the live roses to bring in the house. An amazing thing happened; the bush began to grow, bringing forth more roses. God does the same in our lives, pruning the worthless, dead parts away so we may *live life to the fullest.*

8. **Help a needy family or child**.

This will give you an incredible feeling of pleasure and fulfillment. You may think you are financially unable to help others. However, you will find as you give, God will give back to you.

9. **Send a greeting card**.

In this time of instant messaging, e-mail and cell phones, this may seem such a small action, it isn't worthy of our time. Yet you would be surprised at the reaction of the recipient. My wife has a ministry of sending greeting cards to some ladies at a nursing home. She has done this for several years and finds it very rewarding. Many people face empty days whether in a nursing home, prison, hospital or their own home. No one comes to visit, no one calls, and the mail only brings bills or bad news. Can you imagine what a bright spot in the day a small card brings? The message on the card may be generic, yet the thought comes from the heart. To let them know someone is thinking of them, add a personal note. Why not also include a few lines assuring the person you're praying for them?

10. **Go hunting with a camera**.

Leave your gun at home. You will be surprised how beautiful the world is through the eye of a camera. Study the intricate petals of a flower or the wings of a bird in flight. Get down on your knees; observe the ants, grasshoppers, frogs. Isn't it amazing how God created these tiny creatures? Take a picture of a magnificent deer running through the fields. After printing these photos, you will able to enjoy them for years to come. As for the deer, he will be able to raise his young for your family's enjoyment.

11. Ask God to give or restore your joy of salvation.

Contrary to popular belief, there is great joy in salvation. Knowing God is with us in every trial. We enjoy His watch care for us each and every day. His love for us, and His promise of a home in heaven after this life is over, make each day exciting. All of this and more should give us incentive to look forward to serving Him every day.

12. Close the door to the world.

There is enough clamoring in this world today with phones ringing, TV's running, and computers taking us around the globe. In this day of information, we learn of any tragedy during or seconds after it takes place. There are numerous sports for every day of the week. We have more labor saving devices and less time for the ones who are important to us than any time in history. Why not take a walk through a state park, visit a museum, and go for a drive in the country? Have a picnic in the backyard; if it's raining, have it in the living room. My wife and I did this when we were first married; it is among one of my sweetest memories of those early days.

We have a tendency to become bogged down with many tasks, however we need to realize our work will be there tomorrow when children are grown up and gone. The marriage bond is the most important of human relationship. Neglected spouses grow cold and distant. Many husbands and wives have discovered after the children have departed that they have nothing in common.

13. Pray for others.

We never know the heartaches people experience every day. Become an observer of people. A friend spoke of seeing a woman weeping in McDonald's.

A man with her kept patting her hand, speaking to her, endeavoring to comfort her. The more he tried to comfort her, the more she wept. Perhaps this woman had just lost a child. It is well-known that McDonald's provides Ronald McDonald's Houses to the families of ill children.

Possibly this woman and her husband were experiencing private grief; it may not seem appropriate to approach the family at this time. Yet many welcome an offer to have prayer with them in their time of need. The Billy Graham Association sends out teams to pray with victims who have experienced tragedy. While this may appear to be too little, too late, they are welcomed by the hurting. A few words of comfort can make a world of difference.

14. Share the gospel of Jesus Christ.

There is no greater joy on this earth than to win a soul to Christ, to see their whole life change. Life takes on a whole new outlook, love for family and friends becomes so much sweeter. For the person who accepts Christ, they not only enjoy a new life on earth, but a home in heaven with the Lord for eternity.

In Psalm 126:5-6, God says the one who goes forth weeping shall come again rejoicing, bringing the newly saved with them. Daniel says we shall shine like the stars.

15. Rid yourself of the fear of death.

Are you a child of God? Do you know Christ as your Savior? If so, there should be no fear of death; death just means stepping through a door into a new life. Satan can give false hope while the person is living, yet when they stand at death's door, terror will strike their heart. History is rampant with stories of atheists who scoffed at the thought of God, yet died in distress. How much better it is to settle the question of eternity before you pass from this earth. The Christian should yearn for the time when they can be with their Lord. The troubles of this life will be passed. As we get older, the excitement should build. With each passing day, we are closer to heaven.

Notes

_____

_____

_____

_____

_____

_____

_____

_____

_____

_____

_____

_____

_____

_____

_____

_____

_____

_____

Points to ponder

Are you enjoying today? If not, why not? Are you going through sorrow? Ask others to pray for you. Give your burdens to The Lord. Have you thanked God for this day? Remember God knew about what you're going through before you were born. Each of us faces days of sorrow, the loss of a loved one, financial problems, the sickness of a child, etc. Ask The Lord to help you, and then give your burdens to Him.

Yet if every day is drudgery for you, something is wrong. As stated before and throughout this book, God wants His children to enjoy life. List above the reasons you are not living a full, rich life and how you can change. Analyze your outlook on life in general and your life in particular.

Chapter 5

Take care of yourself.

Body

If you know Jesus Christ as your Saviour, your body is the temple of the Holy Spirit. You wouldn't take an axe to the church building. Nor would you pour beer or wine on the carpet. You wouldn't dare read a Playboy or Penthouse magazine in the sanctuary. Yet Christians do this to their bodies. Christ lives in your heart; your body is more sacred than the most beautiful church building.

Christ said what goes into the eye is what defiles a man. Some have made the statement, 'It's nobody's business what I do to my body." This is the same argument a woman uses who murders her baby through abortion. Yet she who takes the life of another human being is just as much a murderer as one who kills a mature man or woman.

For the Christian, their body isn't their own to do with as they please. It belongs to God for His glory, to praise Him and to bring others into His kingdom. Anything which hinders us from this purpose needs to be eradicated from our lives. Then we can begin to be in harmony with God and live a fuller life.

We are a nation of obese people. This brings us numerous health problems: diabetes, high blood pressure, and heart trouble. Many believe they can't lose weight; with each new diet they become more and more despondent. The testimonies of other's successes only drive them farther into despair.

They give up, believing it may work for others but not for them. There is hope. If you're overweight, first consult your doctor. Before your appointment, write down a list of what you have eaten for the last three days, even if it is a cookie or a handful of peanuts. Take the list with you and show it to the doctor. Is this embarrassing? Yes, however it is necessary. It gives you and your doctor insight into your eating habits. Ask him or her to give you a new list. You'll be tempted to divert from the list for the first week or two, however if you stick to it, you'll find your eating habits changing. When you are tempted, think of how good you will feel after you have shed the pounds. Do it for yourself, not for those around you. Do it for your health. If you try to lose weight so someone else will notice, and they don't see the difference or make a negative comment, it will affect you. However, if you are doing it so you can rid yourself of the diseases associated with obesity; you will have a greater chance of success. Also, many have found the buddy system works wonders for them. Having an overweight friend or partner with you is a great help, so when either of you are tempted, you can encourage each other. When the pounds start to fall off, celebrate even the small victories of a pound or two. However, don't celebrate with food. Finally, see yourself as the person you want to be: slim, trim and healthy, serving our Lord with more energy than you ever imagined.

Mind

Are you careful about where you place your garbage? You certainly wouldn't dump coffee grounds, rotten food and other trash in your children's room. Nor would you leave a loaded gun within the reach of a toddler. A thoughtful, loving parent is always careful of their child's welfare. They want the best they can afford. They wouldn't think of exposing them to something which would harm their health, yet these same loving parents allow their children to watch hours of garbage on TV. The child's mind becomes corrupt by what they see. Then the parents are surprised if the child reacts boldly to his or hers training. Hours of watching disgusting programs take their toll. Our nation's penitentiaries are filled with young people whose parents never thought their child would wind up incarcerated. No one holds a newborn baby in their arms and sees a future inmate in the local jail or prison.

Several years ago I asked the youth pastor of our church what was wrong with the young people today. His answer was very insightful, he stated "The youth of yesterday." After being in the jail and prison ministry for over 27 years, I can attest to the accuracy of this statement. Our churches are empty while our jails, prisons and rehab facilities are overflowing.

Soul

Your soul is the essence of you. The real you, the one no one can see but you and God. When death comes and your body is gone, your soul will live for eternity. Some teach annihilation: that we will die and that this world is all there is. Others believe hell is the grave and some day we all, sinners and believers alike, will live on the same new earth. Tragically, each group who believes this, or other lies which contrast from God's Word, will discover the truth two seconds after they die. They will desire to repent, to turn themselves over to the Lord. It will be too late for them; contrary to popular belief, there is no second chance. If we reject Christ here on this earth, we will face God at the great white throne judgment spoken of in Revelation. There are two judgments; the judgment: seat of Christ is for the believer who has asked Him into their heart. The great white throne judgment is for the ones who never had their sins forgiven.

God desires you to be saved to live with Him for eternity. Your soul is the most valuable part of you. You may have great wealth. Your friends may admire you and want to be like you. But if you lose your soul, you have lost it all. Christ put it this way "For what is a man profited if he shall gain the whole world and lose his own soul? Or what shall a man give in exchange for his soul?"

Your soul is too valuable to take chances. The next breath we breathe may be our last. We never know when our life will end. If you're not already a child of God, why not ask Christ to forgive you of your sin and come into your heart and be your Savior?

Notes

_____

_____

_____

_____

_____

_____

_____

_____

_____

_____

_____

_____

_____

_____

_____

_____

_____

_____

Points to ponder

Are you treating your body like the temple of The Holy Spirit? If not how can you change? Do you have some destructive habit which is damaging your body? Perhaps you need to lose weight. Check with your physician before starting any diet or exercise program. How are you treating your mind? Are you reading, watching or listening to anything detrimental. Is your heart right with The Lord? How can you change? Remember, no one can make you change; you must want to live a better life.

Chapter 6

Fall in love all over again.

Divorce is not an Option.

Today 52% of all marriages end in divorce. Unfortunately, the percentage is just as high among Christians. Couples pass off their dysfunctions with several excuses. We were never meant to be together, we no longer love each other. He/she doesn't support my career, we fight all the time, it's better for the children if we separate, he/she is not a believer. Divorce doesn't happen overnight. No newlywed wakes up the morning after their wedding headed for divorce court. Divorce has become effortless in America. You can destroy your marriage with a do-it-yourself kit; a couple no longer has to travel to Nevada or Mexico. Divorce has not only become commonplace, it is a form of entertainment. Sitcoms, soap operas, and divorce courts draw millions. People ruin their lives in our own living rooms. When I was in grade school, I couldn't name one child's parents who were divorced, now a child would be hard-pressed to name someone whose parents are still married. Christ stated that Moses allowed divorce because of the hardness of men's hearts. It was better to divorce than kill their wife.

God's plan is for one man to marry one woman for a lifetime. Commitment is a marriage where love and romance comes through hard work but it is accomplished. Happy children grow up secure in the knowledge that mom and dad will always be together. Marriage can be a picture of heaven on earth, however, only if couples are willing to work at it. Many celebrities today wouldn't think of getting married without having the other person sign a prenuptial agreement. They plan for their marriage to fail before they ever walk down the aisle. The term is even used *starter marriage*. In most cases when a divorce does occur, the father is the one to leave. Young children can't understand why daddy is no longer there. If he has visitation rights, he becomes a weekend visitor.

He is like an uncle who takes the child on a nice outing, allows them to stay overnight in his home, and then brings them back on Sunday night. They can't cuddle in his arms on weeknights as their father relaxes in his easy chair. They no longer fall asleep in their father's arms to be carried to bed and tucked in by him. For the child old enough to understand, a deep resentment builds. He or she sees mom and dad as a selfish individuals, only thinking of themselves. If the parents use the excuse that it was best for the child, the child feels a deep guilt believing they are the cause for the break up. Assurances to convince them otherwise prove futile. If confronted, they try to hide their feelings.

When another person is brought into the picture, the child feels as if they are a stranger intruding on what's left of the family. Add to this the fact that many times their father has a new family, a new wife with natural children and children from the wife's first marriage. Dad now has new responsibilities with a new son or daughter with which he must spend time. He may try to include the child in activities with the new family. The child may become resentful of the time spent with the other children.

Dad begins to make excuses for missing birthdays, holidays, etc. The children from the first marriage become distant as the gap widens between child and parent. The bottom line is children are devastated. The two people they love, trust, and depend on, refuse to look beyond themselves. After painting such a dark picture, let me hasten to say there is hope.

Marriages can be saved. Children from broken homes can be healed of their mental injures.

This can only come about by the husband and wife trusting in the Lord and making a full commitment first to God, then to each other. I list below some ways to help your marriage. I don't pretend to be an expert. Many writers including John R. Rice, Gary Smalley and others have written many wonderful books on marriage. I suggest you check your local Christian book store or the Internet for good books on rebuilding your marriage. Here is a list of suggestions.

Please understand these will only work if you do them.

1. Pray for your spouse.

Not a quick "Now I lay me down to sleep" prayer, but a heartfelt earnest prayer, for their well-being and any problems they may be facing today.

2. Make a list.

List your spouse's good points, the reasons you fell in love with them. Make a list of their bad points, things they do which irritate you. Take the second list (the one with the bad points) and tear it into very tiny pieces. Dump those pieces into the commode; next, pull the handle. As those pieces are flushed down the drain, feel your frustrations with your spouse drain away. Take the first list (the one with the good points), make copies of it and read it the first thing in the morning and the last thing at night.

3. **When your spouse speaks to you, really listen.**

If the TV is on, turn down the volume. If they are angry, listen for reasons. Don't react with anger, remember the Bible says "A soft answer turneth away wrath." Many times, men may seem to be angry with their wives. Really, they are frustrated with work, expenses, etc. Women may be thinking of problems with the children, the house or work.

4. **Ask the Lord to change them or you.**

This may be a difficult prayer. We want the other person to come over to our point of view. Seldom do we want to conform to their thinking.

5. **Make that person your best friend.**

The one you want to spend 24 hours a day, 7 days a week with. If Joe across the street or Mary at work is your best friend, rethink your priorities.

6. **Tell them you love them.**

Don't be like the Yukon River: frozen at the mouth. Each time you speak to your spouse on the phone, end the conversation with "I love you." Before you go to sleep each night, kiss them and tell your spouse you love them. At first they may respond with silence.

7. **Leave love notes where they will find them**.

A few pages ahead in the book they are reading, in a drawer, include a note with their lunch, etc.

8. **Remember your spouse when you go grocery shopping**.

Do they like a certain food? Women especially like it when their husband is thinking of them. The item doesn't have to be expensive. Sometimes a flower plucked from the garden works just as well.

9. **Be patient.**

Remember it took a long time to get in this position. If you were cleaning and waxing a fine automobile, you wouldn't hurry. You would take your time wanting it to look its best. Your marriage is so much more important than the finest vehicle. Be patient, gentle, kind and understanding. Act as you did when you were dating. It may take some time for your spouse to respond.

Notes

_____

_____

_____

_____

_____

_____

_____

_____

_____

_____

_____

_____

_____

_____

_____

_____

_____

_____

_____

_____

Points to ponder

Make a list of why you fell in love with your spouse. Add to this the good things you like about them. **<u>On a separate sheet of paper,</u>** write her/his bad points, everything you hate about them, any bad habits or actions. Take the sheet with the bad points, tear it into tiny pieces. Now flush it down the toilet. Make copies of the first list, add to it daily. Pray for them; if they will allow you, pray with them. Tell your spouse you love them several times a day. If you are on the verge of divorce, get counseling. If your spouse won't go for counseling, go by yourself. Pastors love to help couples reconcile and save their marriage. If you are already divorced and if you're ex spouse isn't remarried, is there a chance of reuniting? Be respectful of their feelings; don't expect things to change overnight. It took a long time to reach this point. Be patient. Put yourself and your marriage in God's hands.

Chapter 7

Live debt free.

Begin now to live debt free. At the time of this writing, our country is in trouble. The problem is, for the last 30 to 40 years we have been living on credit. For far too long we have borrowed more than we can easily repay. We now live in bigger homes, drive fancier cars. If we have too much, rather than sharing it with those less fortunate, we rent storage units and stuff it with things we will in all probability never use. Now finally, as my father used to say, "The chickens have come home to roost." Our government's solution is to give money to the institutions that made unwise loans. Now the consumers are in trouble. What is the bank's solution? Lend more money, delaying the inevitable. Many hale this as the answer to their problems, not understanding that all they are doing is just delaying the inevitable. It's like wiping down a spider's web every few days. The best thing to do is to kill the spider. Eventually we will run into the same problem all over again; it may be a year, two years or ten years down the road. The next time it will be worse. Any time you delay fixing a problem, be it physical or financial, it will happen again. Procrastination may seem less painful, however, all it does is make the solution more difficult.

One of the greatest sources of stress in a person's life is the amount of money they owe.

Overdue bills, creditors calling at all hours of the day and night, letters from collection agencies and threats of bankruptcy can also destroy a family. To avoid such action, it is better to be proactive. Decide today you aren't going to put yourself in this situation. If you're already in over your head, here are a few suggestions which may help you to become debt free. Understand nothing will help unless you are willing.

1. Speak to your creditors.

Many financial institutions would rather work with you than to foreclose. A lack of communication will only get you further into trouble. Explain your difficulty in meeting payments, ask for their suggestions. Be willing to work with them. If you make an agreement, get it in writing. <u>Be very careful what you sign.</u>

2. Cut up your credit cards.

This may seem too drastic; however for the person who is serious about getting out of debt, it is vital.

3. Analyze what you spend and why.

A compulsion to shop and buy is likely compensation for something missing in that person's life. Perhaps they need the assurance of the love of their spouse or a parent. Keep a record of your spending for one month. Even if you spend a quarter, write it down. You will be surprised what you spend on small items. Where can you cut expenses?

4. Take the extra money saved from cutting expenses and put it on your bills.

Pay off the bills with the highest interest first. After this bill is paid off, take the money saved and pay off the next bill. Depending on your financial condition, this will take some time; however it will definitely be worth it.

5. Shop at Goodwill, second-hand stores, and reduced grocery stores.

Realize you don't have to have name brands. God loves you; His love is more valuable than the finest clothing.

6. A used car is better than a new one.

With the price of new automobiles, you lose several thousand dollars just by driving away from the dealership. Shop around, some cars are owned by people who service them on a regular basis. If the car develops mechanical problems, they have it repaired immediately. These autos are a jewel of a find. There are guides which will show you what to look for when shopping for a used car.

7. Pay off your credit cards.

Just this one accomplishment will bring untold peace of mind. Once they are paid off, resist using them again, you'll be glad you did.

8. Shop grocery stores where the food is discounted.

You will find there is little or no difference in taste. Be prepared to stock up with non-perishables when they are on sale. With perishable items, buy only what you can use in the next week. This will save you from having to throw away spoiled vegetables and in fact throwing away money.

9. Live below your means.

The second job or overtime may seem like the answer to your prayers, however if it takes time away from your family, it's not worth it. Too many people are living in houses they can't afford, driving an automobile which gobbles up their income. A smaller home, a used vehicle is a small price to pay to have time with your loved ones. A loving family is something money can't buy. Whatever age your child is, they will only have one birthday this year. Your wedding anniversary is the most important date on your calendar. Plan a special time away even if it's just an afternoon or evening. Put a few dollars back each payday for this special occasion. Remember no amount of money can replace a spouse or a child.

10. Think before you spend, is this something I need?

Why am I buying this, is it necessary? Can I put off this purchase until I'm in better financial shape? Many times unless it is something necessary for our well-being or those around us, we find the purchase can be delayed.

Notes

_____

_____

_____

_____

_____

_____

_____

_____

_____

_____

_____

_____

_____

_____

_____

_____

_____

_____

_____

_____

Points to ponder

What do you value most in this life? Why are these things
of value to you? Where do you spend most of your time? In
five or ten years, will these things still matter to you? Could
this be your last day on earth? What value do you put on
your spouse, children, and friends? If you lose all your

possessions and all you have left is your family and your God would you consider yourself wealthy?

Chapter 8

To change the world.

Don't quit

Unless it is some destructive habit, the easiest thing to do is quit. We quit our jobs, giving the most asinine excuses. One young man quit because he didn't have enough time to hang out with his friends. As a society, we quit our spouse for any number of reasons. For lack of any other justification, many say they are no longer compatible.

We forget we were not compatible the day we were married. Compatibility isn't automatic; it is learned over a period of years by two people who have made a commitment to each other. We are like the gears of a transmission fitting together. The husband and wife whose marriage survives overlook the other's faults realizing that each marriage goes through rough patches. Reread chapter six with an open mind and heart. As stated before, a family is something which no amount of money can purchase.

A friend who pastors a church in a nearby city was speaking of an incident which happened in a meeting. He 'speaks with his hands' and another man misinterpreted his gestures. He apologized and the incident was smoothed over. Yet there are numerous excuses people use to quit going to church. The pastor is too young, too old. It is raining, snowing, cold, hot, the people are not friendly, and the pastor didn't shake my hand. An elderly lady felt like the pastor should visit her home each week. However if the pastor visits only the homes of the saved and healthy, he wouldn't have time to call on the sick or lost.

A standard excuse for not reading the Bible is misunderstanding the Scriptures. Yet how many could understand a book on engineering or math the first time they read the book. Of course this is ridiculous. It takes careful study of these subjects to master the techniques. Unfortunately many open God's Word, read a few passages, and then declares there are contradictions. They close the most wonderful book in the universe never understanding its truths. For others they understand The Bible all too well, realizing where they will spend eternally.

The Bible takes careful study, comparing Scripture with Scripture, using dictionaries and commentaries from good sound Bible scholars. Regrettably, many will listen to Joe or Jane about spiritual aspects of their lives rather than from an expert. If we have a water leak, we would never think of having a three year old child work on the pipes. Yet we allow those with no knowledge of the things of The Lord to give us advice.

Others quit praying because they see no answers to their prayers. The heavens are brass, nothing is getting through. Yet sometimes God is working in the background, unseen by human eyes.

When the answer comes, we can look back and see the workings of God. God doesn't reveal what or why He does the things He does. If our prayers don't seem to be answered we need to be faithful and wait on Him. Sometimes our prayers seem to go nowhere because of sin, something of which The Holy Spirit convicts us. We may try to gloss it over, or deny it, yet it is always there until we confess and forsake the sin which breaks our fellowship with God. In order to live the best life possible, we must have our hearts right with Him.

A man in jail told the minister who visited him "I'm going to go back" meaning to his old way of life. The preacher asked him. "What are you going back to? The drugs and alcohol which put you here? There is nothing worthwhile to go back to."

Every crew knows that the ship leaving port will face rough seas. The first time a sailor faces a storm it is a frightening experience. The next time he is more familiar with what is required of him. Soon the same sailor will be instructing new recruits on how to face the storms he once feared. God has given us the command to teach others, first the way of salvation, then how to live for Him.

How can we quit from such heavy responsibility? If we don't tell the lost the way of salvation, who will?

Overcoming feelings of inadequacy.

Perhaps you feel inadequate for the task God has laid out before you. If so you are in good company. In Exodus chapters three and four, Moses is arguing with The Lord. His first objection is "who am I and who should I say sent me?" The second is just as lame. As stated before he used his speech as an excuse. God said, "I made man's mouth." Moses learned that God can use any instrument for His glory.

In Judges, the sixth chapter, we read of Gideon, a young man hiding behind the wine press from his nation's enemy. The angel comes to him and greets him with the words; "The Lord is with thee, thou mighty man of valor." How and why could the angel address this young, inexperienced man in such a manner? The reason is because God looks beyond what man sees. He saw a strong person who could and did put the enemy to flight. Gideon starts out with 32,000 men: not a large force considering the number of the Midianites. God tells him to make an announcement; all who are afraid are to go home. Can you imagine how he felt as 22,000 men walked out of camp? It must have seemed as if his entire army had abandoned him. He drew in his breath, stuck out his chest and determined to go on. It would be a tougher battle, nevertheless he would win. The word of The Lord comes to him again. In the test, God selects 300 obedient, trustworthy men who depend not on their own might or skill but on The God of the universe. In the middle of the night, with these 300 men surrounding the camp of the Midianites Gideon breaks the pitchers, blows the trumpet and shouts, "The sword of The Lord and of Gideon." The enemy is routed the victory is won and not a man is lost.

Solomon, as a young king, confessed his need of wisdom to God. He professed his need for wisdom to lead the people in his dominion. As we read the book of Proverbs, we marvel at Solomon's insight. Of course we must realize the wisdom wasn't from education or experience but from the true and living God. Solomon became very wealthy; as a matter of fact, his riches made him a legend. Yet it is his wisdom we celebrate today, wisdom which came not from human understanding; however it come because he put his trust in The Lord.

In the book of Romans Paul speaks of his fight with sin, he concludes by stating his victory only comes through The Lord Jesus Christ.

Peter denied The Lord before a small girl. In the gospel of John chapter 21, Peter declares he is returning to his former profession. He feels he has betrayed The Lord and isn't worthy to be His follower. Christ restores Peter to his former position of leadership and he finds his proficiency in Christ.

Each one of us at some time feels inadequate. You may be newlyweds just starting your lives together or the father looking into the face of his newborn child. Or you may be the pastor who walks into a new church, or the newly appointed boss. Just like the people of The Bible, we have a choice to make: we can try to bolster ourselves with human reasoning or we can rely on The Lord, asking

Him to lead, and guide us in every decision we must make. Asking Him for wisdom.

One program I've found which works very well is to read the book of Proverbs. Starting with the first chapter on the first day of the month and continuing to read a chapter a day until the end of the month. The next month you start over.

In case you think you're alone in this modern age, remember the great novelist Alex Haley. He struggled with feelings of inadequacy and after nine years of working on *Roots*, he was ready to quit. He almost threw himself off a ship into the ocean. While standing on the deck contemplating suicide he heard his ancestors encouraging him to go on. He went back and completed his blockbuster novel.

God has something wonderful for you to accomplish in your lifetime. No one can do it but you.

Maybe there is some dream you've tried to keep hidden all these years. Possibly someone has told that you can't do it or maybe they have even ridiculed your dream. If Henry Ford, Thomas Edison and others had listened to the critics, we would still be walking in the dark.

Study God's Word beginning in the book of Proverbs; ask Him to give you wisdom and direct your path. Let Him have His way in your heart, then you can *Live Life to the Fullest.*

Living for the moment.

Living for the minute has a bad connotation today. Most people believe living minute to minute means not thinking or caring what happens in the future. Not providing for your family, unconcerned where they will spend eternity.

However, for the Christian just the opposite is true. When we realize that we're not in control of our destiny, it frees us of concern for our life. God is in charge of our very existence. The tests and trials we face each day are orchestrated by Him. God doesn't show the future for good reason. If something amazing was going to happen to us tomorrow, we would be in a hurry for this day to pass. However, if something terrible waited for us, with the dawning of a new day we would dread each passing minute. God has veiled our eyes to tomorrow so we will trust Him on a daily basis. When the children of Israel traveled through the desert He fed and provided for them day by day.

We would never have enjoyed the summer of 2007 if we knew that my wife would face a life threatening surgery in January of 2008. With the aorta valve wide open and two other valves in her heart leaking, she was given only a 10 percent chance of survival. All over the world, God's people were praying for her. After a nine hour surgery God brought her through. During her time in the hospital and her recovery, He taught us to trust Him moment by moment. When we lay ourselves and our future in His hands, only then can we truly *Live Life to the Fullest.*

Moment by moment I'm kept in His love
Moment by moment I've life from above
Looking to Jesus till glory doth shine
Moment by moment O Lord I am Thine.

Hymn by Daniel W. Whittle

To change the world.

What will you do in the next 12 months to change your life? When will you start? Do you have the determination to see this transformation come to completion? Of those who decide to quit smoking, only five percent are successful. The average diet only lasts three weeks. If an exercise program lasts a month, it's above the norm. To change the world, we must first change ourselves. Consequently there must be a reason; it's not enough to want the world to be saved. It takes our personal commitment and involvement. If we are not willing to change ourselves we will never see a change in others.

So you say that you want your life to be different? Magnificent, now we are on our way. Begin today. Too many people say "Tomorrow is my day; I'll start tomorrow." Yet when the next day arrives, they find some excuse to put it off. Or possibly the transformation seems so drastic, it appears they are facing a mountain. Yet every mountain can be climbed by taking the first step. Ask The Lord to show you how, and then take your first step today. If you stumble, get back on your feet and go on. Soon you will look back and see how far you came.

When the Communist Party wanted to take over China, their plan was twofold: literature and personal contact. Within a few years, they changed a system that existed for many centuries. If we as Christians want to change the world in which we live, we must do the same. While the purpose of communism is evil, the goal of God's people is divine. Our desire is for those around us to be assured of a home in heaven as well as enjoy life on earth. Throughout this book, we have spoken of the happiness God wants for His people. Can you imagine the joy of spending eternity with those you love? Sometimes our heart becomes hardened because we don't know those we meet on a daily basis. Yet we must remember they are loved by someone. God loved them so much He gave you the opportunity of meeting them. He never does anything by chance; the ones you meet today need your touch. You can change a heart and a life. Many are hurting; they are looking for something to fill the empty space in their heart.

It is said that in the prisons and nursing homes, you will hear weeping in the night. The same is true in many homes in America and around the world. When the lights go out, tears run down the cheeks of countless lonely and discouraged people. God wants to put His arms around them and hold them close to His heart. He can only do this if each Christian does his or her part handing out a small gospel tract, a word of encouragement, a hand on the shoulder as we assure them of our prayers. In this way we can change the world.

Many are dissatisfied with the church they attend. They may find fault with the pastor, the Sunday school teacher, or some other member. They are looking for the problem everywhere but in their own heart. If we want our churches to become vibrant and alive, we must be willing to change ourselves. Volunteer to help in the church, become involved in the visitation program. If there isn't one, start one. Learn to be a soul winner. Study God's Word and the principles of this book. Before long you'll find yourself living life to the fullest.

Live each day as if it were your last.

What if you knew for a fact this was your last day on earth? How would you spend the next 24 hours? Would you call or visit someone with whom you quarreled? How about your spouse? Have you told him/her you love them? How long has it been since you spent time playing with your children?

On that September morning the people working in the World Trade Center didn't know they only had hours to live. Money, houses, automobiles and other possessions lost their value. The climb up the corporate ladder lost its savor. What seemed so vital yesterday was not important when they faced death. Loved ones were called; coworkers huddled together under desks and in stairwells without regard for title or status.

Each one of us are never guaranteed another hour of life. What we do for Christ, for family, friends or neighbors, we must do today.

To live life to the fullest:

I will live this day as if it were my last, viewing it as a gift from God.

I will spend time in prayer to my God, asking Him for guidance in every task, relationship or interaction today.

I will enjoy each moment savoring it as fine chocolate realizing "This is the day which The Lord hath made; we will be rejoice and be glad in it." The trials and temptations I meet today will be of His choosing to make me a stronger person.

I will believe God is still in control even if the world seems to be in turmoil.

I will show forth love to all who are around me, even if they exhibit hostility.

I will put myself in the place of others experiencing what they feel as they go through difficulties in their life.

I will make sure my life is a shining example to those who will follow in my footsteps.

I will exhibit valor in the time of crisis, courage in the face of danger, and compassion to the hurting.

I will realize God made me for this time, for this place. He has work for me to do, winning the lost to Him.

I will realize He only made one of me, and I am of more value to Him than the world itself. I am special to God.

Beginning today, I will live my life to the fullest!

Dear Reader:

It has been my honor to write this book for you. It is my belief that when a person reads a book - novel or non-fiction –their life should be changed for the better. This book should be no exception. I pray this book has transformed your life and along the way, you felt the leading of The Lord. I hope *Live Life to the Fullest* has touched your soul and you enjoyed reading the book as much as I enjoyed writing it. May God richly bless you and may you **Live Life to the Fullest.**

Sincerely

Darrell A. Case

www.ingramcontent.com/pod-product-compliance
Lightning Source LLC
Chambersburg PA
CBHW052215090426
42741CB00010B/2554